The 10 Laws of Transmutation: The Multidimensional Power of Your Subconscious Mind

Dan Desmarques

Published by 22 Lions Bookstore, 2019.

Copyright Page

The 10 Laws of Transmutation: The Multidimensional Power of Your Subconscious Mind

By Dan Desmarques

Copyright © Dan Desmarques, 2019 (1st Ed.). All Rights Reserved.

Published by 22 Lions Bookstore and Publishing House

About the Publisher

About the 22 Lions Bookstore:

www.22Lions.com

Facebook.com/22Lions

Twitter.com/22lionsbookshop

Instagram.com/22lionsbookshop

Pinterest.com/22lionsbookshop

Introduction

The content of this book is seen as a tabu for most people around the world. They even avoid it in their conversations. Because, it address the fundamental laws of life and how it is formed. Without this knowledge, you simply can't understand how this world works or question anything else you learn and get results from most theories on spirituality.

On the other hand, most people are afraid of what others will think of them when expressing their opinions on principles that interfere with existence, namely, in the field of religion, money and politics. In fact, you can lose friends simply by expressing your opinion on any of these topics. And it's precisely because they are so avoided, that so many people need the information that this book will show you. It is for these reasons why should continue reading the following pages.

Money as a Bridge to Better Experiences

Money is the fundamental energy that guides the world and its societies. And naturally, most people want to get more of it to fulfill their desires. They often don't like to talk about themselves when addressing this topic because it interferes with who they are, their goals and their personality. It would be like exposing themselves to others. They don't want to tell how much they earn, how much they need, how much they would like to earn, how much they exactly want for their services or job. And while acting like this, they do admire those who travel, people who are rich, people who have amazing cars, and houses; i.e., they admire material possessions, and even though, meanwhile, they don't want to talk about such things.

On the other hand, it is actually interesting to notice that the nations more open to talk about money, without any prejudice, are also the some of the ones making the most: USA and China. And while the poorest, like Lithuania, Latvia and Estonia avoid it the most.

Another interesting aspect to take into consideration regards appearances and relationships. For while in USA and China people typically value the ones who possess more knowledge and experience, it is in poor countries that you see people being more focused on external demonstrations of wealth, such as the way they dress and the cars they own. And this brings us to the most obvious law of transmutation:

Law 1: Your potential is defined by what you honestly express and seek to understand.

Now what is money? Money is a bridge between the spiritual world and the material world. The choices you make in life, regarding which job you must have, the partner you want to live with, in which country you want to live, if you should or not immigrate to another country, all of these choices condition how much your income will be, because they expose you as well to certain energy frequencies related to it. And quite often, people make choices without realizing how such choices impact them. They may say things like "I don't have enough money" or "my job is not well paid" or "my boss doesn't want to give me a raise" but while saying these things, forget that they, themselves, made all of those decisions, and can only repeat the same outcome with the same mindset.

So many times I have suggested people certain actions that only added more problems to their life, simply because they couldn't understand that my suggestion demanded a change on their mindset. This is the case of one woman who couldn't get a boyfriend: I told her to meet more men to expand her options, and find a more suitable companion. She ended up sleeping with more men. Now she has a pseudo-boyfriend in nearly every country she visits. That's how she sees it, even though they never go beyond sex and empty promises.

The same I could say about a girl I met that was living in a dorm and wanted to buy a house. I told her that if she found a more well-paid job in another country, such as Luxembourg, she could not only buy a house, but rent it and profit from it. Instead, she found another job in her own country, and ruined her career and life, because, well, her boyfriend did not want to live in a poor nation, and ended up leaving the country and her.

Much more I could tell you about stories of people who keep on repeating the same paradigms, and reading things that reinforce their beliefs. Whenever you offer them an option, whatever that is, they take it to reinforce themselves. And so, I have come to understand that the best thing to do for such people is to let them fail. But can they learn upon failing? I have seen women ended up in a hospital bed with health complications and blaming everything except the real cause of it — their alcohol abuse and unhealthy lifestyle. And that's why I often say that the biggest cause of death in the world is stupidity.

Most people aren't dealing with the consequences of their decisions, but avoiding them and avoiding taking responsibility. Their dramas are nothing more than a repetition of thinking patterns that they refuse to change. And when they choose to read a book or make new friends, they choose those who can reinforce exactly the same paradigms they treasure.

How Smart People Create Their Luck

The same principle explained before, applies when people tell others that they are lucky for having more. Many people tell me the same all the time. They say: "I wish I had your lifestyle, because you are so lucky". They forget or neglect, or don't even want to know, how much work I have put in the past to reach the stage where I am now. And surely enough, I have had many women trying to be in a relationship with me just to be able to benefit from my lifestyle, to travel with me, and enjoy a life without working. And how very disappointed they were, when seeing me working from morning to night every single day and telling them that I love to work and love my work. A relationship doesn't last long whenever I make them understand that I will never marry a lazy woman that doesn't want to help me or have a job. And surely enough too, it's painful for me to let go of beautiful women and spend so much time alone every single day, but I don't feel like I have options. The vast majority of the population is asleep, trapped in a mental frequency of enslavement. They do not conceive the world as it is, as a mechanism to which you must contribute and not merely take from.

Law 2: You must give more in order to get more.

It may seem now that I am lucky, in having things that most don't. But they could have the exact same things, or even much more, if they had work as much as I did in the past or still do. Moreover, a big part of my results are obtained because I don't get distracted with superficial things like spending my money in showing to others how much I do that they can't do. Such type of mindset will drive you towards poverty and scarcity sooner than you think. It's always better to work for yourself and for your own life goals. And well, most people will simply not work twenty hours a day, for five or ten years of their life, in order to reach their financial goals, but I've done exactly that.

What is also interesting for me, is that I've seen people doing the exact same things, i.e., working ten hours a day, and sometimes twenty, but for others; I have met people who can spend the entire night working for their company and doing extra hours, often without getting paid, and this, just to guarantee that the process they are working with is completed; so that they can make sure that the company reaches its goals.

If they dedicated themselves as much to a business of their own, as they dedicate themselves to someone else's business, they would now end in a much better financial situation. They could be earning much more. And yet, they do this merely to keep their job, or because the want a raise. But a raise of how much? One hundred, two hundred, five hundred dollars? Quite often their raise is just momentary and not very significant, while such type of raise in any business tends to become exponential, as it means that the company is increasing its profits. But people don't want to accept or even hear this, because it implies something else too: They don't trust themselves as much as they trust their projects. And that's why they humiliate themselves on a job they hate, and then pretend to be proud simply because they are well-paid. In other words, they exchange self-worth for a salary.

Law 3: Never exchange your self-worth for money.

When I was a college lecturer, this was one of the most important things that I always told my students: Never exchange your value for money. And they couldn't understand the point. So I had to peel the layers of this concept one by one. And some, eventually, got it. One student told me he would like to work for a futebol team but had no idea how, as he wasn't a professional player and was merely studying languages. Another told me that she would want to start her own business but had no idea of what to do.

I explained to both that money should not be their priority, but instead, their own value, i.e., the increasing of their market worth when compared to anyone else. And they followed my strategy accordingly. The one who wanted to work for a futebol team offered his time to work as a translator in exchange for nothing in return. He worked for three futebol teams for free, until he finally got the opportunity to work for a British team, earning so much, that he decided to go back to college for a part-time Masters degree.

The other one, built her value by contacting Brazilian companies on what they needed from their trips to China, then built a traveling plan as I suggested, divided in three packages; and she made so much money, that she was able to employ other people, and then focus her time on a new business, creating her own coffee shop franchise, while earning from the first business on tourism.

This principle is so multidimensional that most people don't even see how they already possess the opportunities they seek. For example, once I met a receptionist of a hotel that told me she often travels to Georgia because she loves the country. She said that she would like to travel more, but with two jobs, as a receptionist and teacher, there wasn't enough free time. And so, I told her to create a travel agency focusing only on Georgia. She initially claimed that not many people would be interested because the country isn't popular. But I told her that what seemed like a barrier was just an even better opportunity for her, as there was not enough competition. And so, she tried the idea, it worked, and that's her business now. She was able to quit her other two jobs after only a couple of months.

Why Knowledge Isn't Enough to Make You Rich

Hardly, you will get paid much more than the salary you stared with in a job. And yet, you could get this raise just by working on one of your ideas; simply by having followers, a newsletter, and promoting products, which don't even need to be products created by yourself. You can easily start a business selling someone else's products, even from home, merely using affiliate marketing, digital or physical products, a website, and working from anywhere, or a local coffee shop, in your spare time. That profit, from such part-time business, can be the extra income you need and even turn into your salary one day. But most people forget this, when begging for a raise, or seeking for more part-time work to increase their monthly financial income. And I call it begging because it is how it is seen by the owner of the company. And that's why many experts say that it's easier to get a raise by simply changing your job. It's actually easier to negotiate when you join the company than much later. But why so many people can't change? Well, because they don't trust themselves enough. And this trust has nothing to do with knowledge, even though it seems that information improves the capacity of a person to do something.

When I was living in Spain, a friend asked me for ideas to make profit. I told him: Well, as a Spaniard, with a degree in Economy, a nice car, and plenty of experience in your own country, it would be a great idea to sell villas. And so, he contacted some agencies, got the contracts, but, that's all he did. He never promoted anything online, because he simply did not trust his capacity to sell. He got lazy and abandoned the idea.

At the same time, another friend of mine, a refugee from Nigeria, also living in Spain, asked me for my opinion on selling Villas. I told him that the idea was great, and also told him about that other guy that was wasting his time waiting for someone to guess that he wanted to sell villas, and recommended him to use market research and social media, to promote the houses. Since then, he is making a very good profit and constantly inviting relatives to spend holidays with him in Spain. He travels much more than ever to Africa and back to Spain.

He understood that everything requires a belief. But that may also be the main difference between him and the Spaniard, as the Nigerian was a very dedicated Christian.

Law 4: All knowledge is subservient to belief and actions matching it.

As you see, money is truly a bridge in your life. You are constantly depending on it to cross somewhere, depending where you need or want to go. It's a bridge made of decisions, made of perspetive and based on patterns. It's how we see the world that conditions how much money we make.

To illustrate the previous explanation, days ago, a very naive girl told me that money isn't the only way to define a culture, showing me how ignorant she is. Because you see, everything, absolutely everything inside a culture, is defined by money. So much that I can always tell that whoever hates the rich and says that money is a luxury, is certainly poor. And I am always right. Once, another girl told me: "Money is not important". And to this I promptly replied her: "That's why you don't earn much". And she admitted it to be true, and living in a small room, not even apartment, adding that she barely can afford it. After that, she went into a rant about how miserable her life is and how much more she would like to have. I am not even surprised that she was attracted to me and not the other poor losers in the group. Because I was the only one who seemed to live a wealthy lifestyle and not need to worry about money.

I have to say, these people, women or men, are hypocrites, because they say one thing but want another. Their mouth is not where their thoughts lay. And it's this lack of honesty that drives their existence into chaos. Because they are repeating the mantra "money is not important" to calm themselves down from the horror of waking up every day to a life they hate, and at the same time, they are seeking for opportunities they can't find and a spouse that can rescue them from the hell they created for themselves with their own mindset.

I once had a girlfriend that was beautiful but mentally broke, and quite stupid too. When I found that she was living with a gay man, I invited her to share an apartment with me. I was still looking for one, so I told her to wait until I found one she wanted. I sought to find the exact apartment she wanted. And this miserable girl, had very high expectations indeed. She was sharing a dorm with another man, and yet, she wanted a house with a big living room, a very nice kitchen, in the center of the city, with a balcony. After nearly two months looking for one matching all she wanted, I found it. When she arrived on the first day, she said: "I can't believe you found this amazing house".

Well, yes, she demanded it and then couldn't believe I got it. I did add to her: "With me you will always get things you considered impossible, and you just need to enjoy it."

I was being honest, because I could have married her and she would not have to work any more for the rest of her life. Instead of that, what did she do? She tried to cheat on me, flirted with other men in front of me, and then proceeded to insult me and arrive home drunk all the time. When I told her we couldn't live together anymore, she tried to remove me from the contract. And well, it was when she put things at this level, that I had to remove her out of my life. She was challenging me and asking for a war, and she got it, and lost it. Everyone supported me, including her own family. And she lost the house, and ended back at sharing a house with that gay man. Now, this stupid loser, continues to go around in circles in her life, trying to find a man that wants her, and not understanding why nobody likes her except for a one night of sex; but that's her real worth: one night.

You see, most people overprice themselves too much. They are not worth what they want. They are very far from it most of the times. So never expect to make someone of poor value, overpricing herself, match your expectations. Because they won't.

Law 5: Don't buy promises from cheap people overpricing themselves.

Why You Shouldn't Overlook Honesty

There are many cases of people telling me that money is not the most important thing in life, and then asking me for a job in one of my companies. And well, if money doesn't matter to them, why do they even need me to pay them? I would be happier if they worked for free.

Some people may make more and others less, but at the end, everyone is somehow simply chasing money, and molding their character, beliefs and choices, accordingly, namely, in regarding what they need, want and can get. They are so obsessed with this triangular application, that they will use permanently, when making friends and even seeking for a spouse. The strong egotism and need, and poverty mindset, leads them to a mental pressure, of constantly asking themselves, whenever they meet someone: What can I get from this person? Does he/she has what I need? Do I want it?

More than ever, people now are so driven by their own desires, that they don't even socialize anymore unless having something to gain. I know that, whenever men see me with a beautiful girlfriend, they all want to be near, to learn from me. It's when I share the knowledge with them, that they then disappear. The same applies with women to whom I offer books. Once they get the information, they forget who gave it. Sometimes they will even organize seminars, as I have seen, sharing the information with others as if it belonged to them, never ever inviting me and much less quote me. Because they are ashamed of what I would see if I was there. But that's how disgusting most people truly are.

Now, obviously, I don't expect art students or teachers to ever tell me that money is very important, because they can't live with the idea that they'll likely never earn much during their entire life. Besides, the most unsuccessful painters I ever met, are demotivated, because nobody buys their vast amount of pantings that they stock in their house. The same thing happens with the many teachers I encounter that hate their job but have no idea of what else to do with their life, because that's what they studied for and all they can do.

Most people are also too lazy, because you always need to make sacrifices to earn more, among which restarting a new career is certainly the most challenging. A less challenging one would be to change country, in order to find a better position, as either a teacher or a painter. And that's why I say that most people are too lazy, as they don't even want to leave their country and friends behind. And yet, I have met painters from Ukraine making a lot of money in Belgium, teachers from Great Britain getting rich in China, Hong Kong, Malaysia and Macao, and also accountants from Lithuania making more money than they ever imagined possible in London. So may never anyone say that a salary depends on a job. It doesn't; It depends on where you are.

Law 6: Personal wealth is exponential to location and relative to the ratio between need and supply for what you can offer in that same location.

Why Money Can Buy Love

I know that I could be making much more money than I do now. But I also made choices according to what I learned, and I've set other priorities in my life, and I chased other dreams before too. And actually, in many points, I can say that I reached my goals recently, namely, the one of being retired. The only reason why I don't remain retired, is because I want to make more money and I love what I do. But I did enjoy one year without working at all in the past.

Now, at some moments in my life, I was, as I still feel, lost. But I don't really regret anything, not even wasting my money eating outside every single day in countries like Denmark, Poland and Belgium, and just being lazy at the beach in Span all by myself, while listening to podcasts. That's certainly when I understood the value of love, but as I say to friends: I can't just go in the supermarket and buy a package of love. Neither can I try to pick a girlfriend from the shelf of that supermarket. I also can't just approach a woman and ask her if she wants to live with me for the rest of her life. Well, actually I can, but socializing in today's world is quite a headache, with people constantly judging you and everything you say. On the other hand, most women nowadays either think that I am totally insane, or just out of their league, which in this case doesn't mean not being very handsome, but traveling too much for what they seek — which is a man that stays at home and helps them go through their boring life.

Most people are extremely bored, and that's why they are always spending money in partying, drugs and weekend holidays. They have no idea of what to do with their time. And so many times, I had quarrels in my relationships, because my girlfriends had nothing to do and were bored as hell. Women get bored easily, and that's fine. The problem is when they think that my time only becomes useful when addressing their needs, and at same time complain that I don't make enough money to travel with them when they want. Even if that was the case, I wouldn't pay for a woman to take a jet plane by herself to another part of the world where I couldn't see what she was doing.

Furthermore, the two things don't work well together: You are either making money or wasting your time. And if you wan't both, you need to sacrifice years of your life.

Now, how many years would such women sacrifice to be able to finally get married with me and then spend the rest of their life just raising children and chilling at the beach with a coconut in their hands? I tell you: zero. Not even one weekend. Most women want the Ferraris, Porches, mansions and castles to magically appear. They don't care where they come from. That's why some women I met, who did not even believe I make money legally, have told me: "I don't care if you are doing something illegal; I would still be with you."

That's how much women care about having a relationship with a criminal. It is fine as long as the criminal is rich, and takes them to party on a boat, and helps them fill their social media with pictures they can show to their friends, proving that they are moving upwards in life. That's how they see their value. Surely not all, but enough to keep me single until my 40s. I am not married because I can't find a woman to get married, and not because I have money to enjoy my life and live as I want, without working. Women don't want poor men with plenty of free time. So let's not assume that all those cliches we see and read and hear all the time are true. The large majority of the world is simply lying to itself. People lie when they tell you that money can't buy happiness. Their happiness certainly depends on money, and the less they have, the more it will be so.

Law 7: If you don't think money can buy happiness, you don't know where to shop.

How to Unlock Your Potential

I'm perfectly aware that I am responsible for my choices and, as so, my results too. I am happy with the life I have now. And that's also why I don't work so hard anymore. I can set new goals and achieve more, but going back to what I said previously, it's all about a personal decision. I know what I need to do, how many hours of work I have to apply, what I have to create and how to get my goals. And I always do everything with specific techniques that guide me there. I will now be sharing them all with you.

Imagine what you want to create: I do this by closing my eyes, and imagining a group of people in front of me. I then proceed in verbalizing what I did and how. The how doesn't really matter, as this is just an exercise for the imagination. The energy produced with the exercise is what truly matters. Everything I say is related to what I want. So, if you want to get married, you would say: "...and I married this woman, who is like this and that, and does this and that."

Meditate with emotions and mantras: I close my eyes, and sit in a lotus position or any other, with my back straight, every morning and every night; and then I use specific mantras accompanied by epic music or joyful music to motivate me, while I repeat such mantras. The music helps me with my emotions and visualizations. The mantras are related to what I want, and I start them all with "I have now...", or "I am grateful for..." or "thank you for...".

My favorite mantra is: "I love having... and that loves me". For example: "I love money and money loves me"; "I love my wife and my wife loves me"; "I love my life and my life is full of love for me". This principle applies to everyone who wants to become wealthy and happy because you can only manifest that to which you offer love.

Law 8: Love and appreciate what you want in order to manifest it in your life.

Handwrite a list of ten things, every morning, starting in the past tense with "I achieved" and regarding all the things you want. I write this list every day, and toss in the trash after finishing. It's the habit of writing that keeps me tuned.

Listen to your own voice: Do this by repeating what you want for yourself. I will record myself saying: "You have..." and then proceed to add what I want to achieve. The brain can't tell the difference, and because the voice is familiar, your own voice, you will attract what you want much faster. I often use my full name, in order to create a more powerful effect. And I then listen to this audio three times a day, with my earphones, or as if it was a call received from myself. Nobody needs to know and you can even set an alarm clock that sounds like you are really receiving a call, to make sure that you do this every day. Take it as medicine, during meals — morning, lunch, and dinner.

That's how I take responsibility for my decisions but many people I encounter don't. They want the money but don't want the work that comes with it; they are not interested in helping others or providing useful service, or even in repeating these exercises. And that's why they remain poor. Then, however, these same individuals see others who have more as lucky. But they're not lucky. They're just more responsible. They worked hard, used the law of attraction and disciplined themselves to reach their goals, rather than wasting their life chasing frugalities and nonsense theories about spirituality. Many people even chase more popular authors instead of me, because, well, they know me, and they think an imbecile that spread garbage on youtube is more important than me, who gains his knowledge from the most secretive religious organizations in the world, with thousands of years of existence. And well, I can't beat that logic; I can't win in any discussion with a fool. I always lose such debates. Arguing with a fool is a complete waste of time.

Law 9: Never argue with a fool because he will fool you into wasting your time.

The concept of money as a bridge, is also a reflection of something internal, for the bridge is found within you. It depends on how you're made — wood or stone. It depends if you have or not any bridge within you. People without education, for example, who don't even read a book, have no bridge in their life, and want to jump to the other side with the lottery or some other magical method. That's exactly what their type of thinking and words show. The fact that many even believe I do illegal things to earn my money and to have the lifestyle I enjoy, shows how stupid they truly are. Truly, the greatest mistakes I ever did in my life was to waste my time in trying to understand the fools and the idiots of society. This is why I must tell you to focus only on your goals and never get distracted with the superficial illusions of the world or what you hear from others: Focus on what you want and never allow yourself to get distracted from reaching it, and you will certainly get there, for that is the ultimate law above all laws previously mentioned, and that unites them at the same time. This is also the only reason why you should meditate. Everything else, should match your results in the physical world, and not the outcome of your meditation practice.

Law 10: Master your emotions and your mind and you will master your life.

The 10 Laws of Transmutation

Law 1: Your potential is defined by what you honestly express and seek to understand.

Law 2: You must give more in order to get more.

Law 3: Never exchange your self-worth for money.

Law 4: All knowledge is subservient to belief and actions matching it.

Law 5: Don't buy promises from cheap people overpricing themselves.

Law 6: Personal wealth is exponential to location and relative to the ratio between need and supply for what you can offer in that same location.

Law 7: If you don't think money can buy happiness, you don't know where to shop.

Law 8: Love and appreciate what you want in order to manifest it in your life.

Law 9: Never argue with a fool because he will fool you into wasting your time.

Law 10: Master your emotions and your mind and you will master your life.

About the Publisher

This book was published by the 22 Lions Bookstore.
For more books like this visit www.22Lions.com.
Join us on social media at:
Fb.com/22Lions;
Twitter.com/22lionsbookshop;
Instagram.com/22lionsbookshop;
Pinterest.com/22LionsBookshop.